GW01237706

# Everyone's OK!

### Keith Gaines
### and
### Tessa Krailing

Nelson

# Contents

# A bad day for Ben and Mr Belter

Mr Belter was looking at Ben's book.
'This is not very good, Ben,' said Mr Belter.
'I'm afraid you will have to do this again.'
'Yes, Mr Belter,' said Ben.
Mr Belter went on.
'And this is really terrible.
You will have to do all of this again.'
'OK, Mr Belter,' said Ben.

Mr Belter slammed Ben's book shut.
'And I don't like to hear anyone saying "*OK*" in
my classroom,' he said crossly.
'OK, Mr Belter,' said Ben.
Mr Belter looked more cross.
'Oh, sorry,' said Ben. 'I wasn't thinking.
I shouldn't have said "*OK*".
I'll try to remember not to say that.'
'No, Ben,' said Mr Belter quietly.
'You *will* remember not to say that!
Now do this again, and this time
do it much more carefully!'

At the end of the day, Ben had still not finished.
Today was Monday.
Every Monday, some of the boys in Mr Belter's
class did football training after school.
'Right,' said Mr Belter.
'You lot can all get ready for football.'
Mr Belter came over to Ben.
'Let me see your book,' he said.
Mr Belter looked at Ben's book.
'I haven't finished it yet,' said Ben.
'Well, you'd better finish it now,' said Mr Belter.
'Don't come out to football until it's all done!'

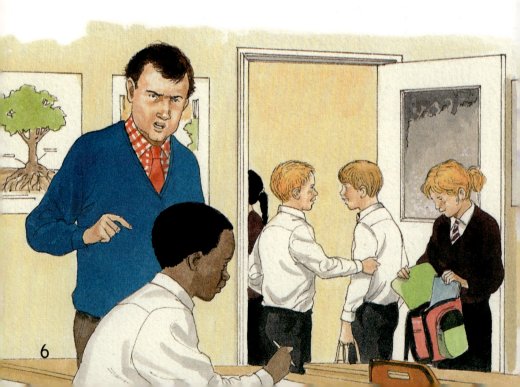

At last, Ben finished and he went
out of the classroom.
When he got outside, he saw that the football
training had just ended.
Ben was really cross about missing it.
He went back to the classroom to get his bag.
The caretaker and a cleaner were
cleaning outside the classroom.
'Be careful,' shouted the caretaker.
'It's wet. You would not like it if you slipped.'
Ben got his bag and walked back out.
The caretaker shouted again.
'Now look. You've left foot marks all
over where I've just cleaned!'
Ben slammed the door behind him.

Ben was always upset at being told off.
'Mr Belter has told me off today,' he thought,
'and the caretaker's told me off as well.'
He was glad to get home.
It had been a bad day.
But now Ben was watching TV.
It was his favourite show.
The police had closed in on the mad gunman.
They had almost caught him.

'I'm not scared of you,' shouted the gunman.
'You'll never get me, anyway.'
'Come out with your hands up!' shouted the police.
The gunman lifted his gun.
'Bang! Bang!'

'What's all this noise?' asked Ben's Dad.
'That television is far too loud.
I can't think with all this noise going on.'
Ben's Dad switched off the television.
'Don't switch it off now,' shouted Ben.
'I have to see if the police get the mad gunman.'
'Look, Ben,' shouted his Dad.
'You have your own television in your room.
Go and look at it there – and shut the door!'

Ben raced upstairs to his room and
switched the television on.
He couldn't wait to find out what had
happened to the mad gunman.
But Ben had missed the end.
It had finished.

# A new friend

'This is a very bad day,' Ben thought, as
he pulled on his coat.
'Mr Belter and the caretaker were
cross with me at school.
Dad is cross with me at home. I'm going out.'

Ben walked slowly over to the park.
He took his football with him.
He thought about going to see Rocky or Wing Chan,
but he didn't really feel like it.
He'd play on his own.
As Ben walked into the park,
he saw a dog standing by the gate.
'Hello, dog,' said Ben.
'What are you doing here?
Are you waiting for someone?
I haven't seen you before,
and I don't think you live in the Square.'

'You look unhappy,' said Ben.
'Is it because you are all on your own, like me?
What are you called?' asked Ben,
'and where's your home?
There is no name on here to tell me.'

'Come on, dog,' said Ben.
'We'll just get cold, standing here all night.
Let's do some running to get warm.
You can do some football training with me.'
Ben and the dog played football all over the park.
Ben started smiling and the dog wagged its tail.
They had both found a new friend.
'I feel like something to eat,' said Ben.
'Let's see what we could get.'

Ben and the dog looked in the
window of the Chinese take-away.
'Shall I go in here, or shall I go to
the fish and chip shop?
What do you think, dog?' asked Ben.
'Would you like some noodles or some rice or
some bean sprouts?'

The dog just looked at Ben.

'Well, would you like some chips?' asked Ben.

'Woof, woof!' went the dog and
it jumped up at Ben and wagged its tail.

'Oh, you like chips, do you?' said Ben.

'OK, we'll go and get some chips.'

# Chips for Chips!

Ben bought some chips.
'Here you are, dog,' said Ben.
'You can have some of my chips.
Don't you like eating Chinese food?
Do dogs find it difficult to eat with chopsticks?'
Ben watched as the dog kept eating the chips.
'You like eating chips, don't you?' said Ben.
'I know. That's what I shall call you.
I shall call you Chips!'

Ben was just clearing up the rubbish when
Rocky and Max came along.
'Hello, Ben,' said Rocky.
'Where did you find that dog?'
'I found him in the park,' said Ben.
'I've never seen him round here before,' said Rocky.
'What's his name?'
'I don't know what he was called before,
but I think I'll call him Chips,' said Ben.
'Chips, say hello to Max.'
'Woof!' said Chips. 'Woof!' said Max.

'Chips is like me,' said Ben.

Rocky was surprised and he laughed.

'How can Chips be like you?' he asked.

'You haven't got four feet and you haven't got a tail!'

'Chips is all on his own.

I am all on my own, too,' said Ben.

'I don't have any friends.

That's why Chips is like me.'

'That's stupid,' said Rocky. 'I'm your friend.

Tony and Tessa and Jamila and Wing Chan
are your friends.

You've got lots of friends.

And now Chips has a new friend.'

'It's getting dark,' said Rocky. 'We have to go now.
I'm sure you'll feel better in the morning.
I'll see you tomorrow. Come on, Max.'

On the way home, Rocky met Ben's Dad.
'Hello, Rocky,' he said. 'Have you seen our Ben?
He seems to have gone missing.'
'Yes, he's back there,' said Rocky.
'He's in the park, playing with a dog,
and I think he's feeling unhappy.
He thinks he doesn't have any friends.'

Ben's Dad was worried. Why was Ben upset?

'There you are, Ben,' said his Dad.

'I was worried about you.

You've been out a long time.

Who is this?'

'This is Chips. He's my new dog,' said Ben.

'I found him. He's really friendly.

Will it be all right if I keep him?'

'First, we must find out who owns him,' said Ben's Dad
'Someone may be looking for him.
They may be worried about him.
They may be missing him as much as I missed you.
Before we take him home, we'd better take him to
the police and see if they know anything about a
missing dog.'

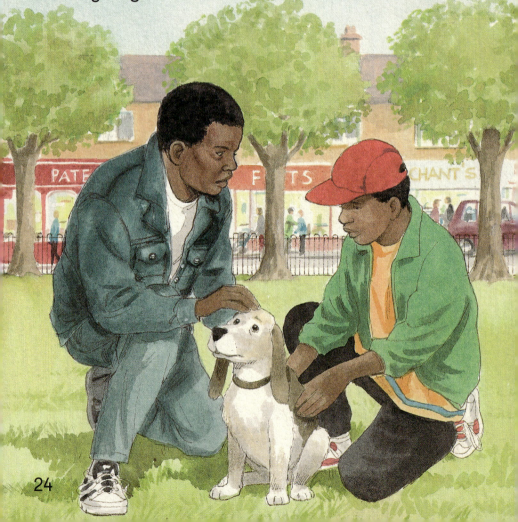

They took Chips to the police.
An old lady was talking to the policeman.
She looked unhappy.
'I took this off to let him have a good run around.
One minute he was there and the next
minute he was gone.
He's never run away before.
I'm sure something terrible has happened to him.
He is a lovely dog. I can't think where he can be.'

She looked around as Ben and Chips came in.
Suddenly, she shouted,
'Ben, you bad, bad boy.
Where have you been?
I've been so unhappy without you.
Why did you run away, Ben?'

Ben didn't know what to say.
He didn't know the old lady at all.
He was sure she didn't know him.

But Chips remembered the old lady.
Chips ran over to her and jumped up at her.
The old lady looked very happy to see him.
The old lady spoke to the policeman.
'Here he is,' she said.
'Here is my dog. Here is my lovely Ben!'
The dog had the same name as Ben!

# Ben goes home

The old lady was smiling, now that
she had found her dog.
Ben wasn't smiling.
He had wanted to keep Chips, but
now Chips was with the old lady.
And Chips wasn't called Chips anyway.
He was called Ben.
Ben the dog went home with the old lady.
Ben the boy went home with his Dad.

Ben's Dad saw that Ben was unhappy.
'You had to let Chips go,' he said.
'He wasn't yours and he had to
go home with the old lady.
Did you see her face?
She was so pleased to get her dog back.'
'Yes, that's true,' said Ben.
'The old lady missed her Ben, just as I
missed my Ben,' said his Dad.
'Let's go home and watch television.
You can have the sound as loud as you like!'
'OK, Dad,' said Ben.

The next day, Mr Belter looked at Ben's book again.
'This is much better, Ben,' said Mr Belter.
'I can see that you've really tried hard to
get these right.
Just do these next three, then you've finished.'
'O...' said Ben.
Ben was just about to say, 'OK, Mr Belter,'
but he remembered what Mr Belter had said.
Mr Belter looked at Ben.
'Oh what?' said Mr Belter.
'Oh, good!' said Ben.
Mr Belter smiled.

Later, Rocky spoke to Ben.
'How are you today,' asked Rocky,
'and how is Chips?'
Ben told Rocky all about how they had
taken Chips to the police, and
how the old lady had taken Chips home with her.
'Anyway, I'm OK now,' said Ben,
'and the old lady and the dog are OK too.
Mr Belter was pleased with what I did this morning,
so he's OK.
Everyone's OK!'
Just then Kevin ran by with a football.
'Out of the way, stupid,' shouted Kevin crossly.
'Well,' laughed Ben, looking at Kevin.
'Nearly everyone's OK!'